JB SEQUOYAH
What's your story,
Sequoyah? /
Shaffer, Jody Jensen.
33341005674246

CUB REPORTER
MEETS FAMOUS AMERICANS

WHAT'S YOUR STORY,
SEQUOYAH?

Jody Jensen Shaffer
illustrations by Doug Jones

Lerner Publications ◆ Minneapolis

Note to readers, parents, and educators:
This book includes an interview of a famous American. While the words this person speaks are not his actual words, all the information in the book is true and has been carefully researched.

Lerner Publications Company
A division of Lerner Publishing Group, Inc.
241 First Avenue North
Minneapolis, MN 55401 USA

For reading levels and more information, look up this title at www.lernerbooks.com.

Main body text set in Avenir LT Pro 45 Book 15/21. Typeface provided by Linotype AG.

Library of Congress Cataloging-in-Publication Data

Shaffer, Jody Jensen.
 What's your story, Sequoyah? / by Jody Jensen Shaffer.
  pages cm. — (Cub reporter meets famous Americans)
 Includes bibliographical references and index.
 Audience: Ages 5–9.
  ISBN 978-1-4677-8786-4 (lb : alk. paper) — ISBN 978-1-4677-9651-4 (pb : alk. paper) — ISBN 978-1-4677-9652-1 (eb pdf)
  1. Sequoyah, 1770?–1843—Juvenile literature. 2. Cherokee Indians—Biography—Juvenile literature. 3. Cherokee language—Writing—Juvenile literature. 4. Cherokee language—Alphabet—Juvenile literature. I. Title.
E99.C5S3884 2015
973.04975570092—dc23 [B]   2015027316

Manufactured in the United States of America
1 – VP – 12/31/15

Table of Contents

Hello, everyone!
Today I'm talking with a very special person. His name is Sequoyah. Sequoyah, can you tell us about yourself?

Sequoyah says: Certainly. I grew up in a **Cherokee** community in what is now the southeastern United States. My people lived off the land by farming and hunting. I did not go to school. I spoke Cherokee, not English. My people did not have a written language. When I got older, I created a system of writing Cherokee words. I taught the Cherokee how to read and write. It was the first time Cherokee stories and history had ever been written.

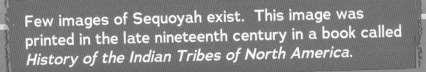

SE·QUO·YAH.

Few images of Sequoyah exist. This image was printed in the late nineteenth century in a book called *History of the Indian Tribes of North America.*

When and where were you born?

Sequoyah says: I was born between 1760 and 1770 in a small village in modern-day Tennessee. I don't know the exact date. My mother, Wu-te-he, was a full-blooded Cherokee. I'm not sure who my father was. He didn't live with us. Some say he was a man named George who was half Cherokee and half white. Sometimes people called me George too. I lived with my mother and brothers. We all worked very hard caring for the cattle and the garden on our land.

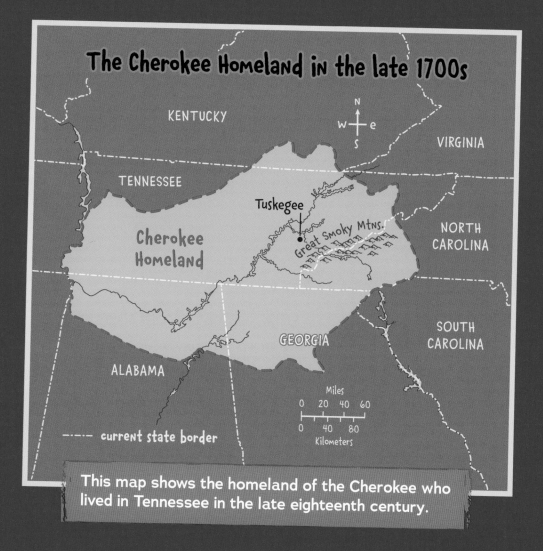

The Cherokee Homeland in the late 1700s

KENTUCKY

VIRGINIA

TENNESSEE

Tuskegee

Cherokee Homeland

Great Smoky Mtns.

NORTH CAROLINA

GEORGIA

SOUTH CAROLINA

ALABAMA

Miles
0   20   40   60

0   40   80
Kilometers

-·-·- current state border

This map shows the homeland of the Cherokee who lived in Tennessee in the late eighteenth century.

What was your childhood like?

Sequoyah says: It wasn't easy. From the time I was small, I suffered from bad swelling in my knees. My knees hurt all the time. I walked with a limp. I often couldn't run with the other children. But I loved to play in the woods. I also kept busy helping my mother. She had a trading business. She traded tools and weapons for furs. While she worked, I helped out around our home.

This print from 1777 shows American Indians in Canada trading furs with Europeans.

Furs like these were valuable to traders in Sequoyah's time.

What were your interests as a young man?

Sequoyah says: When my mother died, I took over her trading business. I also learned to be a silversmith. I made beautiful plates, jewelry, and vases. I wanted to sign my work. I'd seen white silversmiths do that. But the Cherokee didn't have writing. I told some of my friends about how I'd seen white men writing things down on paper. My friends thought the writing had to do with **witchcraft**. They told me to forget what I'd seen. Yet I didn't want to forget. Instead, I wanted to learn more! I began to think about how Cherokee words could be written.

Silversmiths use tools like these to create silver jewelry. Sequoyah learned how to make beautiful jewelry and other objects out of silver.

What was your life like when you got older?

Sequoyah says: In 1813, I joined the US Army. They were fighting the Creek, another group of American Indians. The fight was over who would control a large area of land. While in the army, I saw the white soldiers reading and writing letters to their families. I wanted to do the same. I decided then and there to make an alphabet for the Cherokee.

The Creek War took place between 1813 and 1814. The war ended at the Battle of Horseshoe Bend. Sequoyah fought alongside white soldiers under General Andrew Jackson.

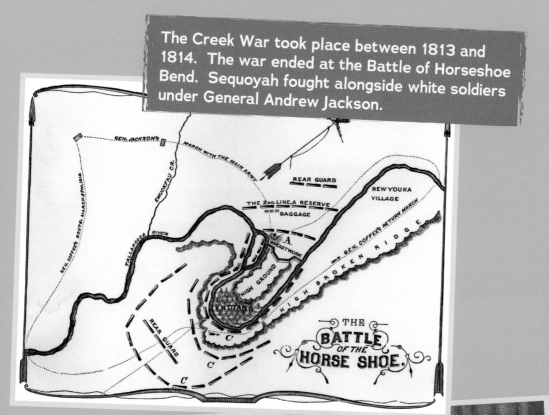

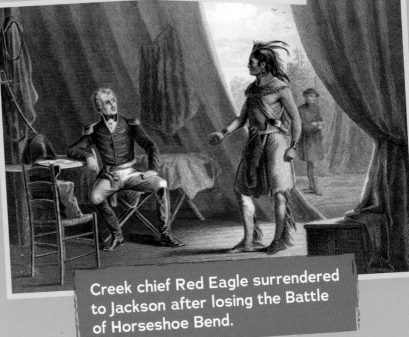

Creek chief Red Eagle surrendered to Jackson after losing the Battle of Horseshoe Bend.

How did you create a Cherokee alphabet?

Sequoyah says: I started by giving each Cherokee word a symbol or a picture. Then I realized there were too many words to do that easily! So I listened to how people spoke. I created a symbol for each sound I heard. It took me many years. In 1821, I ended up with symbols for eighty-five **syllables**. By putting syllables together, I could write words. I had created a **syllabary** instead of an alphabet. I taught my young daughter, A-Yo-Ka, to read and write using my method. She loved it! But not everyone was happy with my invention.

Cherokee Alphabet.

a	e	i	o	u	v
D a	R e	T i	Ꭳ o	O u	i v
S ga Ꭷ ka	Ꭸ ge	Y gi	A go	J gu	E gv
Ꭹ ha	Ꭾ he	Ꭿ hi	F ho	Ꮁ hu	Ꮂ hv
W la	Ꮄ le	Ꮅ li	Ꮆ lo	Ꮇ lu	Ꮈ lv
Ꮉ ma	Ꮊ me	H mi	Ꮋ ni	Ꮌ mu	
Ꮎ na Ꮏ hna Gꭴ nah	Ꮑ ne	Ꮒ ni	Z no	Ꮔ nu	Ꮕ nv
Ꮖ qua	Ꮗ que	Ꮘ qui	Ꮙ quo	Ꮚ quu	Ꮛ quv
Ꮝ sa Ꮝ s	4 se	Ꮟ si	Ꮠ so	Ꮡ su	R sv
Ꮣ da Ꮤ ta	S de Ꮤ te	Ꮧ di Ꮨ ti	V do	Ꮪ du	Ꮫ dv
Ꮬ dla Ꮭ tla	L tle	C tli	Ꮰ tlo	Ꮱ tlu	P tlv
Ꮳ tsa	V tse	Ꮵ tsi	K tso	J tsu	Ꮸ tsv
Ꮹ wa	Ꮺ we	Ꮻ wi	Ꮼ wo	Ꮽ wu	6 wv
Ꮿ ya	B ye	Ꮵ yi	Ꮶ yo	Ꮽ yu	B yv

Sequoyah created symbols to represent syllables used in the Cherokee language. This chart shows these symbols.

Why were people unhappy with your writing system?

Sequoyah says: Some people thought the system was witchcraft. They didn't trust it because they had never seen a Cherokee write before. They brought my daughter and me before the town chief, George Lowery. He asked some warriors to hear my case and judge me. If I had been found guilty, I would have been killed. The warriors created several tests. They separated A-Yo-Ka from me. They told her what to write. I read it back to them. Then they told me what to write. A-Yo-Ka read it back. The warriors decided my symbols stood for Cherokee words, not witchcraft. Soon many in my village learned how to write and read.

George Lowery was the leader of the Cherokee village where Sequoyah lived.

How did your system spread beyond the village?

Sequoyah says: In 1822, I traveled to a spot along the Arkansas River where Western Cherokee lived. I taught the Western Cherokee my syllabary. The next year, my family moved to the area. I was made a member of the General Council. In 1824, the General Council of the Eastern Cherokee—the group of Cherokee to which I'd originally belonged—awarded me a medal for my invention. I received it a couple of years later because I was busy traveling. I wore my medal every day for the rest of my life.

Sequoyah wanted to spread his writing system. He traveled to a site along the Arkansas River *(below)* where the Western Cherokee lived and taught them his system.

Did anyone else help spread your writing system?

Sequoyah says: Yes. A man named Samuel Worcester helped. He was a Christian **missionary**. In 1825, he ordered **type** and a printing press. He wanted to **translate** the Christian Bible into Cherokee. In 1828, the *Cherokee Phoenix* was printed on the printing press. It was the first Cherokee newspaper. Many people learned my syllabary and read this paper. One thing they read about was white settlers. They wanted us to move west so they could live on our land. In 1828, I went to Washington, DC, with other tribal leaders. We signed a **treaty**. We exchanged our land for land in what is now Oklahoma.

Samuel Worcester wanted to spread Christianity. He translated the Bible into Cherokee.

The *Cherokee Phoenix* newspaper was a way to share news and information among the Cherokee.

What happened after you signed the treaty?

Sequoyah says: I moved west with my family the year after I signed. Hundreds of other Cherokee moved west too. I built a log cabin and learned to be a blacksmith in the West. But many Cherokee stayed farther east. President Andrew Jackson didn't like that. He wanted all the Cherokee to move way out west. My people were upset. Many of us had helped Andrew Jackson by joining the US Army and fighting against the Creek. Those forced to move were angry that Jackson wanted them to go so far away from their homes. President Jackson ended up forcing the Cherokee to move. Approximately sixteen thousand Cherokee were made to head far west. Many died on the trip. It became known as the **Trail of Tears**.

Native peoples, including the Cherokee, were forced to move from their homes.

How did the Cherokee Nation change after the Trail of Tears?

Sequoyah says: Things were very hard for us. The Eastern Cherokee and the Western Cherokee all lived together after the Eastern Cherokee were forced to move. Each group wanted to do things its own way. And each group thought it should be in charge. But I encouraged everyone to try to get along. They took my advice. We were able to avoid a war between the groups. I was elected president of the Western Cherokee, and I kept encouraging people to work together.

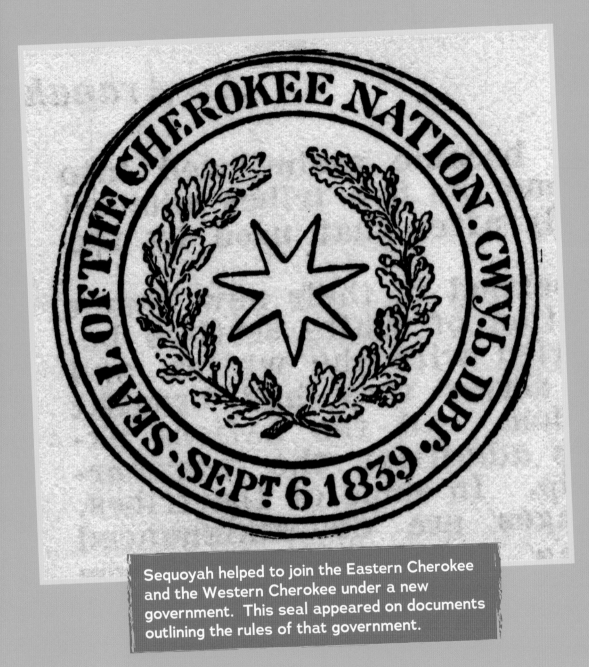

Sequoyah helped to join the Eastern Cherokee and the Western Cherokee under a new government. This seal appeared on documents outlining the rules of that government.

How did you continue encouraging the Cherokee to work together?

Sequoyah says: Well, I wanted all the Cherokee to live as one. I heard there was a band of Cherokee in Mexico. They had left the East many years earlier. I wanted us to all live together, so I traveled all the way to Mexico to find them. Things didn't go quite as I had planned in Mexico. I found the Cherokee. But they preferred to stay in Mexico. Still, I was proud that I'd reached out. And most of all, I was proud that I'd created a community in the West made up of Eastern and Western Cherokee.

Visitors to Tennessee's Sequoyah Birthplace Museum can learn more about Sequoyah's many accomplishments.

How did the lives of the Cherokee improve because of you?

Sequoyah says: My system of writing and reading gave people a new way of communicating. It also allowed our stories, history, and culture to be widely shared. My system changed the lives of the Cherokee forever. In fact, my syllabary is still used by the Cherokee today.

Timeline

1760   Sequoyah is born around this time in what is now Tuskegee, Tennessee.

1813   Sequoyah joins the US Army and fights against the Creek.

1815   Sequoyah marries Sally Waters and begins working on his syllabary.

1821   Sequoyah is tried and found innocent of witchcraft.

1824   Sequoyah receives a medal from the General Council of the Eastern Cherokee for his syllabary.

1828   Sequoyah signs a treaty exchanging his people's land for land in modern-day Oklahoma.

1829   Sequoyah moves to modern-day Oklahoma.

1838   At least sixteen thousand Cherokee are forced to move west on the Trail of Tears. More than fourteen hundred Cherokee die on the journey.

1843   Sequoyah dies while traveling in San Fernando, Mexico.

Glossary

Cherokee: American Indian people originally of Tennessee and North Carolina

missionary: a person sent on a religious mission to spread Christianity

syllabary: a system of writing in which each character represents a complete syllable

syllables: the parts into which a word is divided when it is spoken out loud

Trail of Tears: the name for a journey in which at least sixteen thousand Cherokee were forced to leave their homes and go west

translate: to express in words the text of another language

treaty: a formal agreement between two or more people or groups

type: printed letters, characters, or symbols used in a printing press

witchcraft: the practice of magic by use of spells

LERNER

Expand learning beyond the printed book. Download free, complementary educational resources for this book from our website, www.lerneresource.com.

SOURCE

Further Information

Books

Coleman, Wim, and Pat Perrin. *Sequoyah and His Talking Leaves: A Play about the Cherokee Syllabary*. South Egremont, MA: Red Chair, 2015. Check out this picture book and reader's theater script to learn more about Sequoyah.

Levine, Michelle. *The Cherokees*. Minneapolis: Lerner Publications, 2007. Learn more about the Cherokee people's history and culture.

Wade, Mary Dodson. *Amazing Cherokee Writer: Sequoyah*. Berkeley Heights, NJ: Enslow, 2009. This biography tells Sequoyah's life story.

Websites

Cherokee Colors
http://www.learnnc.org/lp/multimedia/11574
Learn how to say the names of some colors in Cherokee at this fun site.

Cherokee Foods
http://www.learnnc.org/lp/multimedia/11575
Once you've learned some Cherokee colors, visit this site to learn to pronounce the names of foods!

Oklahoma Historical Society: Sequoyah's Cabin
http://www.okhistory.org/sites/sequoyahcabin
Read about Sequoyah's cabin in Oklahoma and discover more facts about his life.

Index

Photo Acknowledgments

The images in this book are used with the permission of: Library of Congress, p. 5; © Laura Westlund/Independent Picture Service, p. 7; © Rolf Hicker/All Canada Photos/ Getty Images, p. 9 (top); © Peter Newark American Pictures/Bridgeman Images, p. 9 (bottom); © Agencja Fotograficzna Caro/Alamy, p. 11; © North Wind Picture Archives/Alamy, pp. 13 (top), 15; © MPI/Getty Images, p. 13 (bottom); © Mike Junio/George Catlin/Wikimedia Commons/(cc 1.0), p. 17; © Don Smetzer/Alamy, p. 19; Courtesy Wikimedia Commons, p. 21 (top); © American Antiquarian Society/Bridgeman Images, p. 21 (bottom); The Granger Collection, New York, p. 23; © CORBIS, p. 25; © Jerry Whaley/Alamy, p. 27.

Front cover: Library of Congress.